Q. What did the paper say to the p[encil?]

A) Write on!

Q. What do you call a fairy that doesn't like to shower?

A) Stinkerbell!

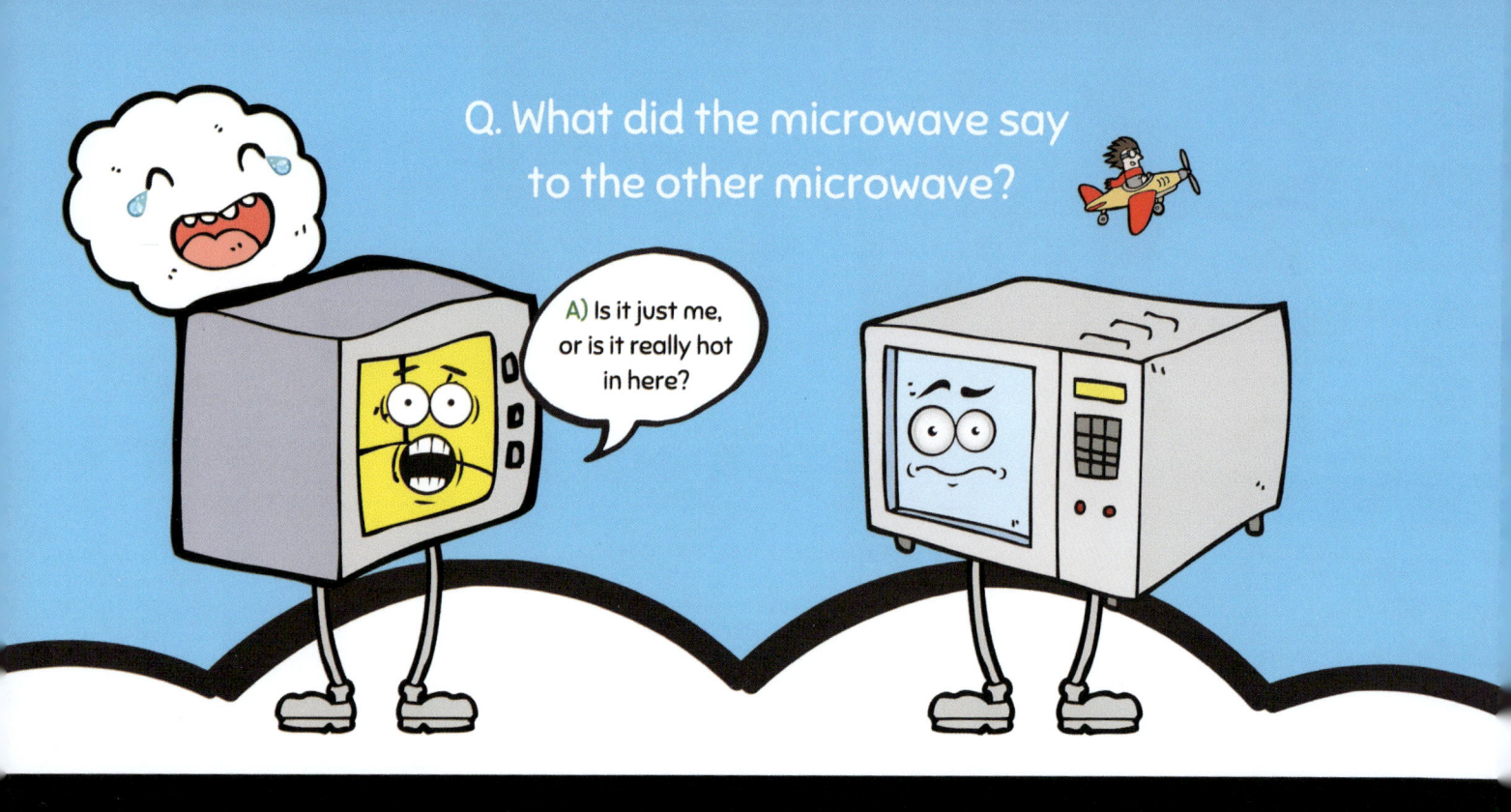

Q. What did the microwave say to the other microwave?

A) Is it just me, or is it really hot in here?

Q. What is a pirate's favourite letter?

A) Arrrrrrrrr!

Q. How do you make a milk shake?

A) Give it a good scare!

Q. Where do cows go on Friday nights?

A) To the Moo-vies!

Q. What did the toilet say to the other toilet?

A) You look a bit flushed!

Q. What did the man say to the pack of cards?

A) I'll deal with you later.

Q. What did the fridge say to the other fridge?

A) You want to chill?

Q. What kind of keys are sweet?

A) Cookies!

Q. Why do the French like to eat snails?

A) Because they don't like fast food!

Q. Why did the banana go to the doctor?

A) Because it wasn't peeling well!

Knock, knock.
Who's there?
Water.

Water who?
Water you waiting for? Hurry up and let me in!

Q. What is a cat's favourite colour?

A) Purrrr-ple?

Q. Why did the chicken cross the playground?

A) To get to the other slide.

Knock, knock.
Who's there?
Dishes.
Dishes who?
Dishes the police, open up!

Q. What is orange and sounds like a parrot?

A) A carrot.

Q. What do you call a dog that goes to a beach in the summer?

A) A hotdog!

Q. How do they answer the phone in the paint shop?

A) Yellow?

Q. Why did the animals in the zoo stop taking spelling tests

A) Because it was full of cheetahs.

Knock, knock.
Who's there?
Dozen.
Dozen who?
Dozen anybody want to let me in?

Q. How do you make the number seven even?

A) Remove the S.

Q. What makes music in your head?

A) A hair band!

Q. What vitamin helps you see?

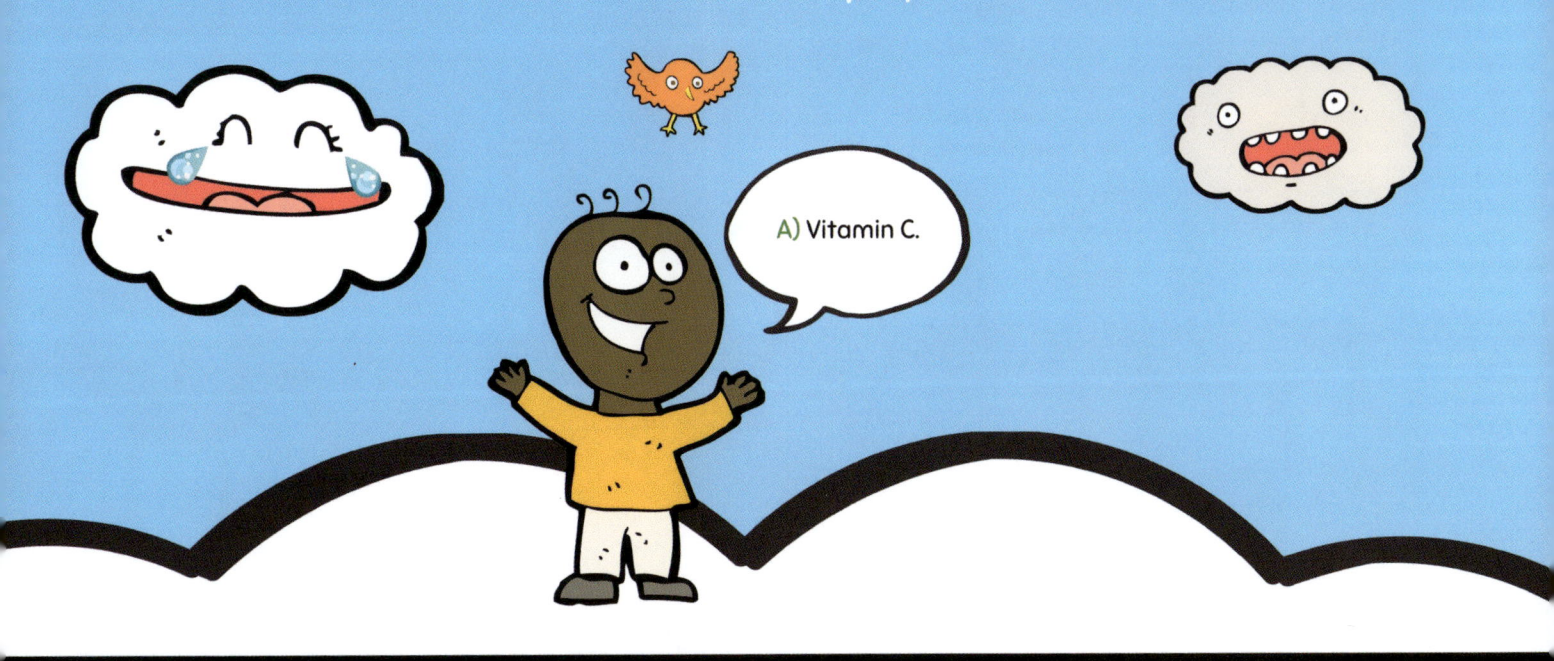

A) Vitamin C.

Q. What animal do you want to be when your cold?

A) A little otter!

Q. Why couldn't the strawberry cross the road?

A) Because he'll cause a traffic jam!

Q. What do you call someone with no body or nose?

A) Nobody knows.

Q. What's brown and sticky?

A) A Stick, silly!

Q. What do you call two bananas on the floor?

A) Slippers!

Knock, knock.

Who's there?

Doris.

Doris who?

Door is locked, that's why I'm knocking!

Q. What do you call a sleeping bull?

A) A bulldozer.

Q. What do you call an old snowman?

A) Water!

Q. What do you call a sleeping dinosaur?

A) Dino-snore!

Q. What type of key opens up a banana?

A) Mon-keys!

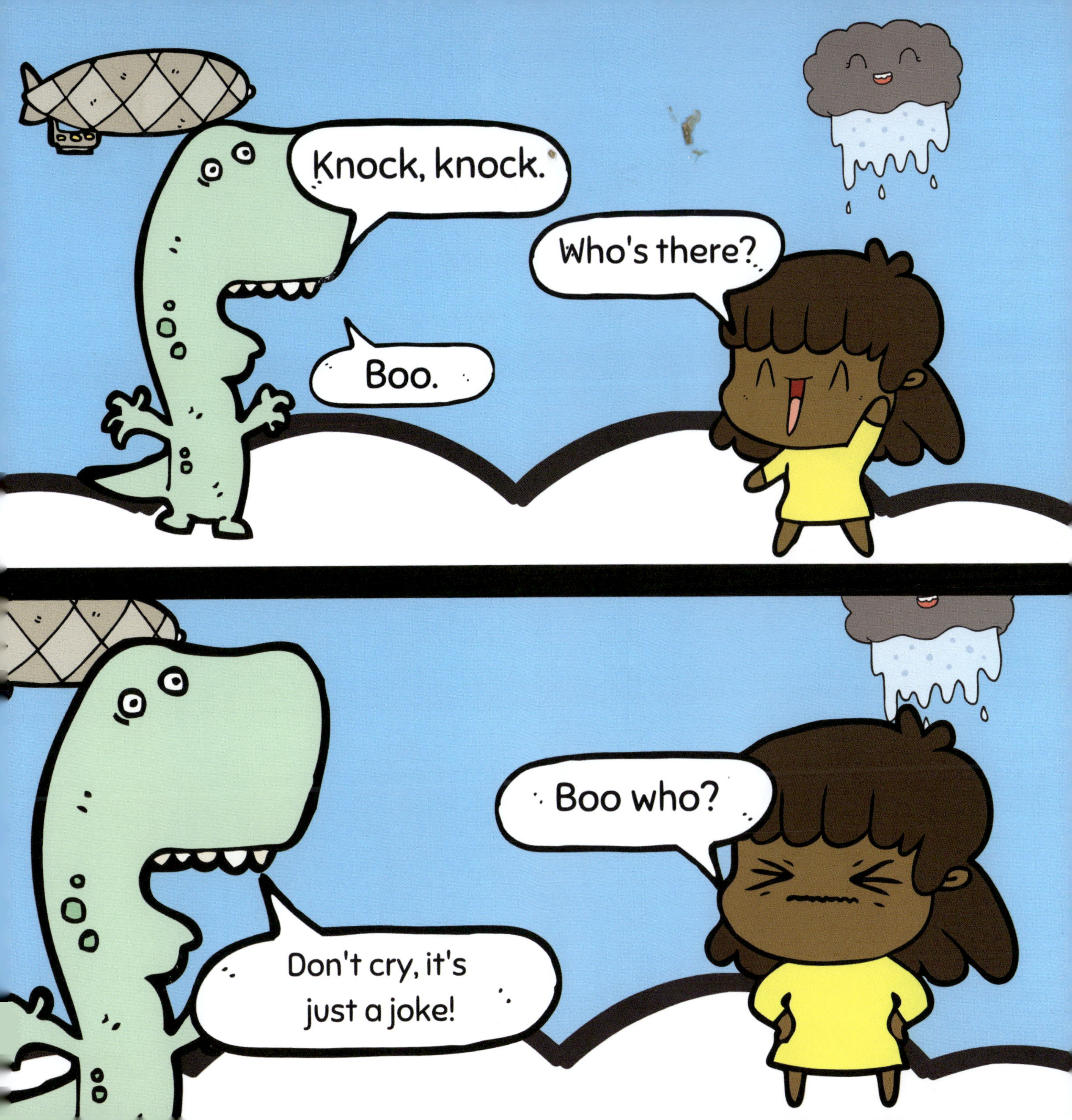
Knock, knock.
Who's there?
Boo.
Boo who?
Don't cry, it's just a joke!

Q. Why did the farmer jump on his potato plants?

A) Because he wanted to make mashed potatoes!

Q. Why did the puppy do so well at school?

A) Because he was the teacher's pet!

Q. What do you call a sheep with no legs?

A) A cloud!

Q. What did the triangle say to the circle?

A) Your pointless!

Q. What are the richest fish in the world?

A) Goldfish!

Q. What did the big flower say to the tiny flower?

A) Hey bud!

Q. What music frightens balloons?

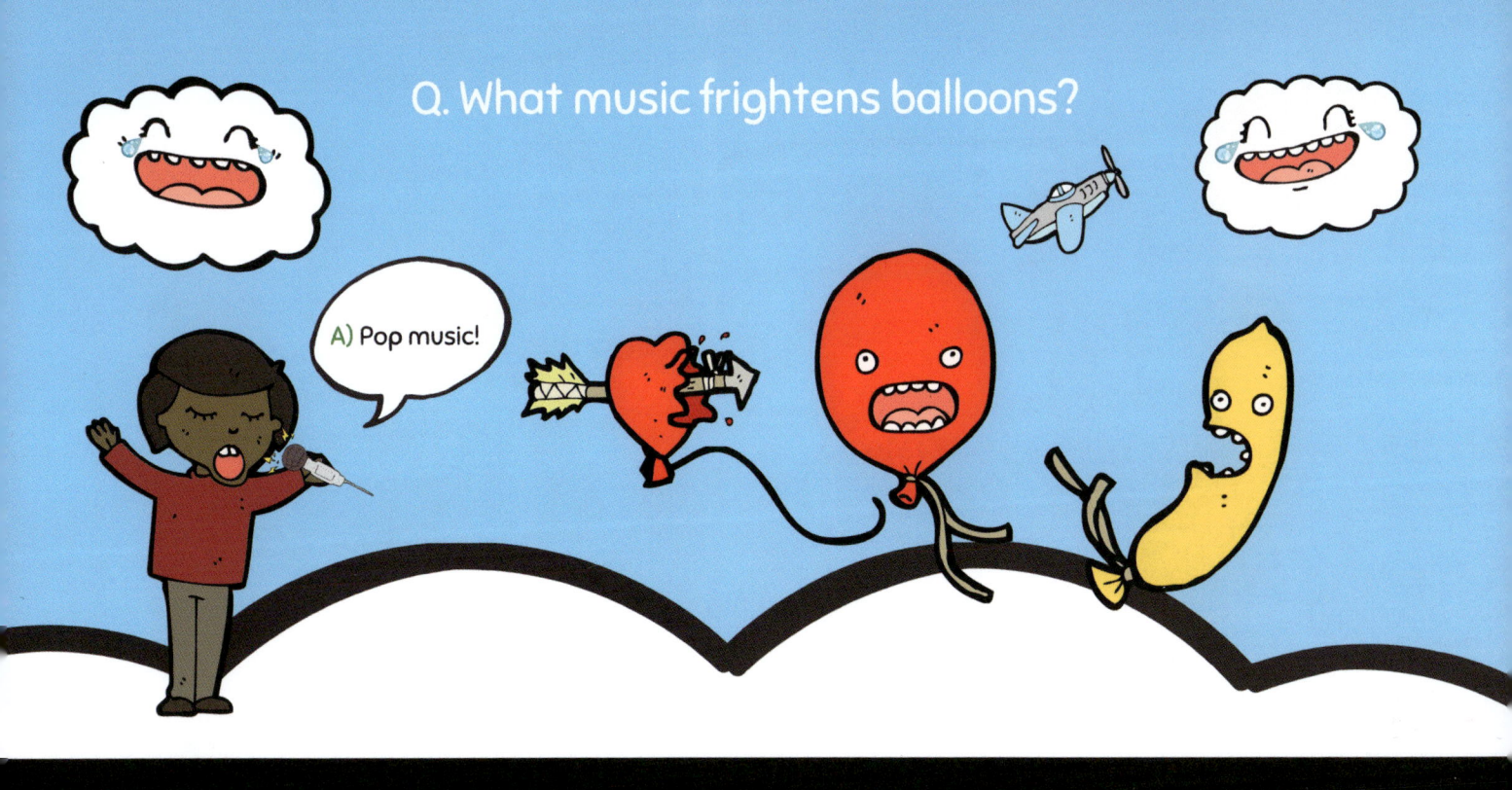

A) Pop music!

Q. What is a witch's favourite school subject?

A) Spelling!

Knock, knock.
Who's there?
Donut.
Donut who?
Donut ask me, it's a secret!

Q. What do you call a dancing lamb?

A) A baaaaaaa-lerina!

Q. Why was the man running around his bed?

A) He was trying to catch up on some sleep

Knock, knock.
Who's there?
Ben.
Ben who?
Ben knocking on this door all morning!

Q. Why is 6 afraid of 7?

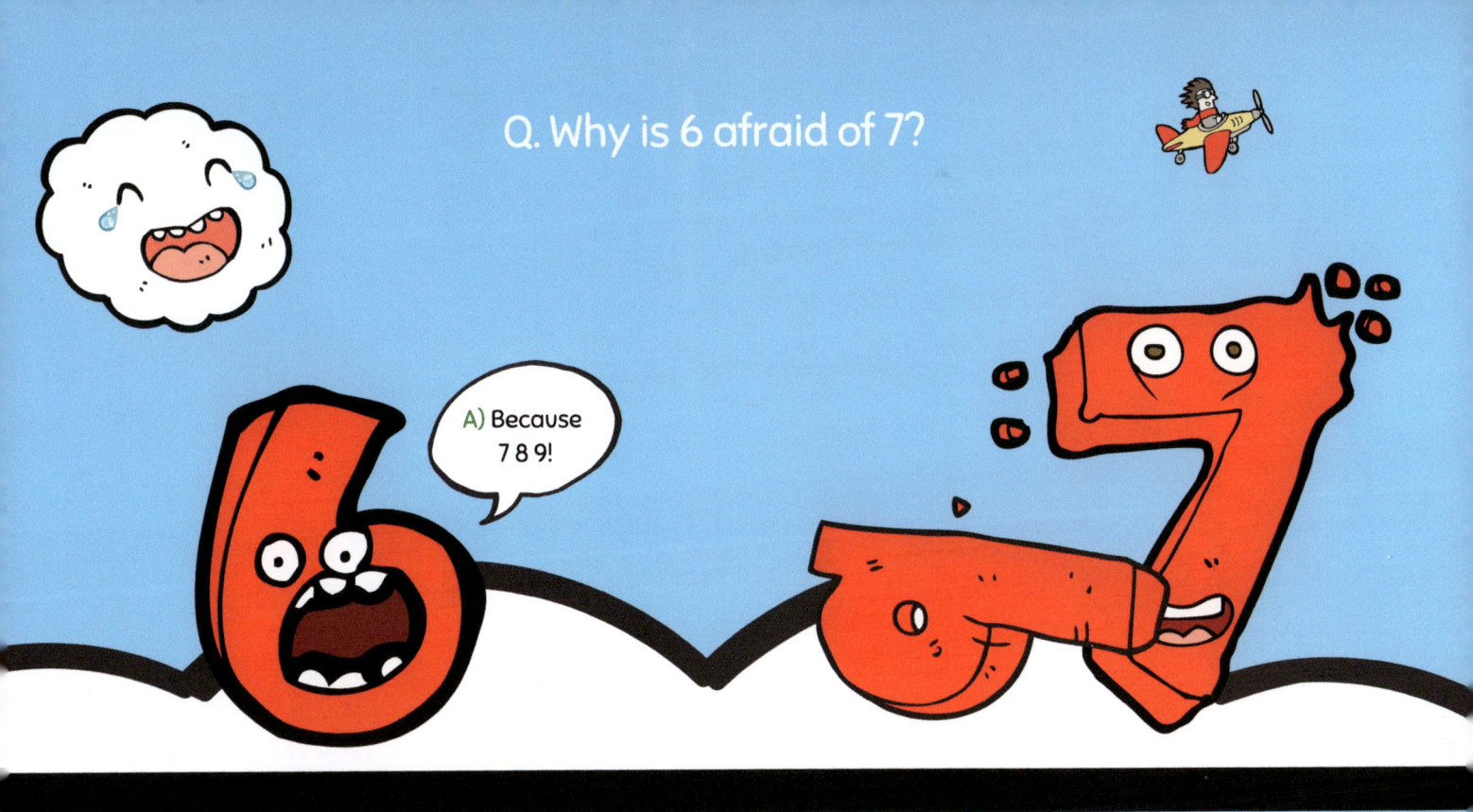

A) Because 7 8 9!

Q. How did the barber win the race?

A) He had a shortcut!

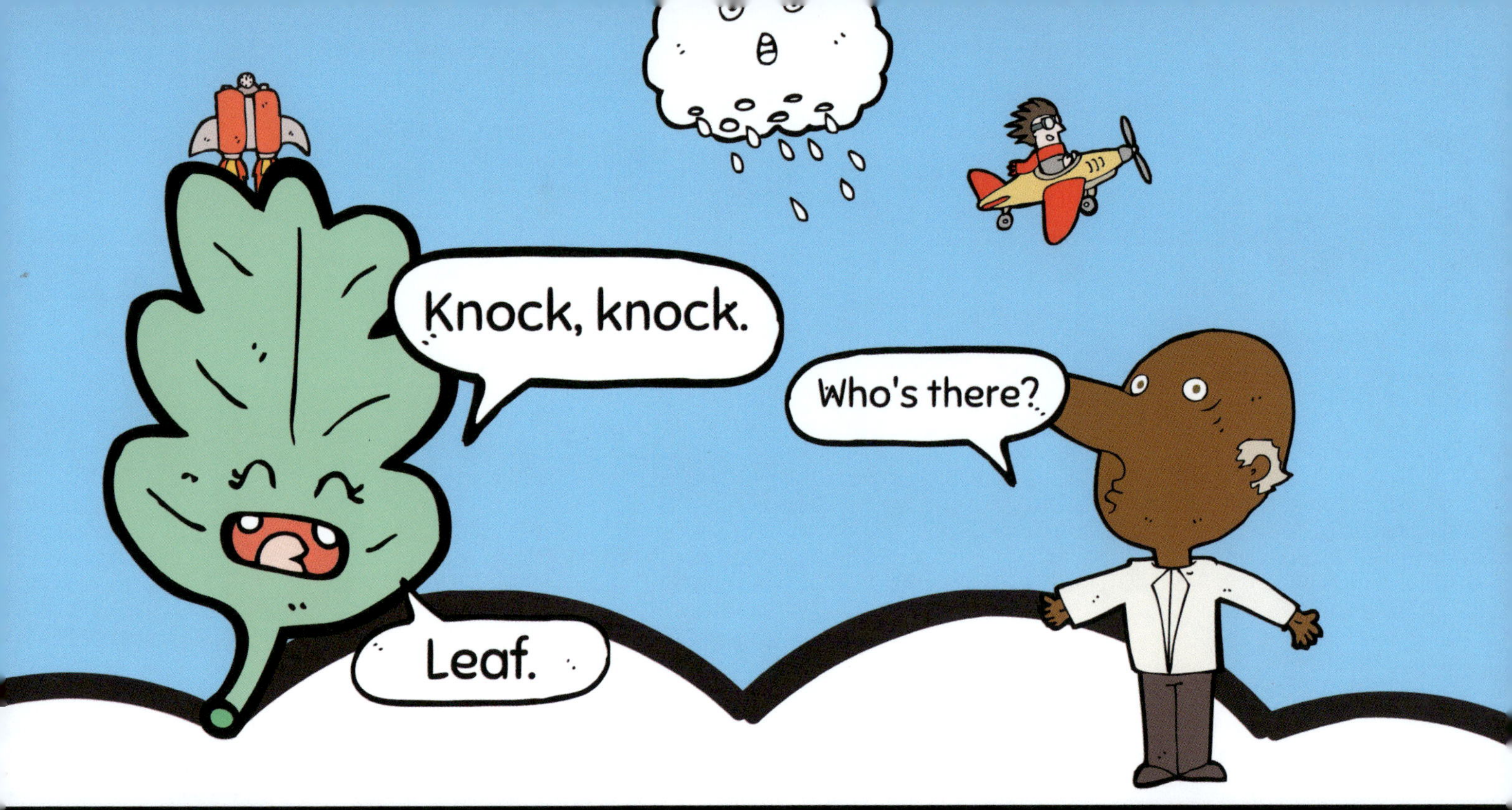
Knock, knock.
Who's there?
Leaf.

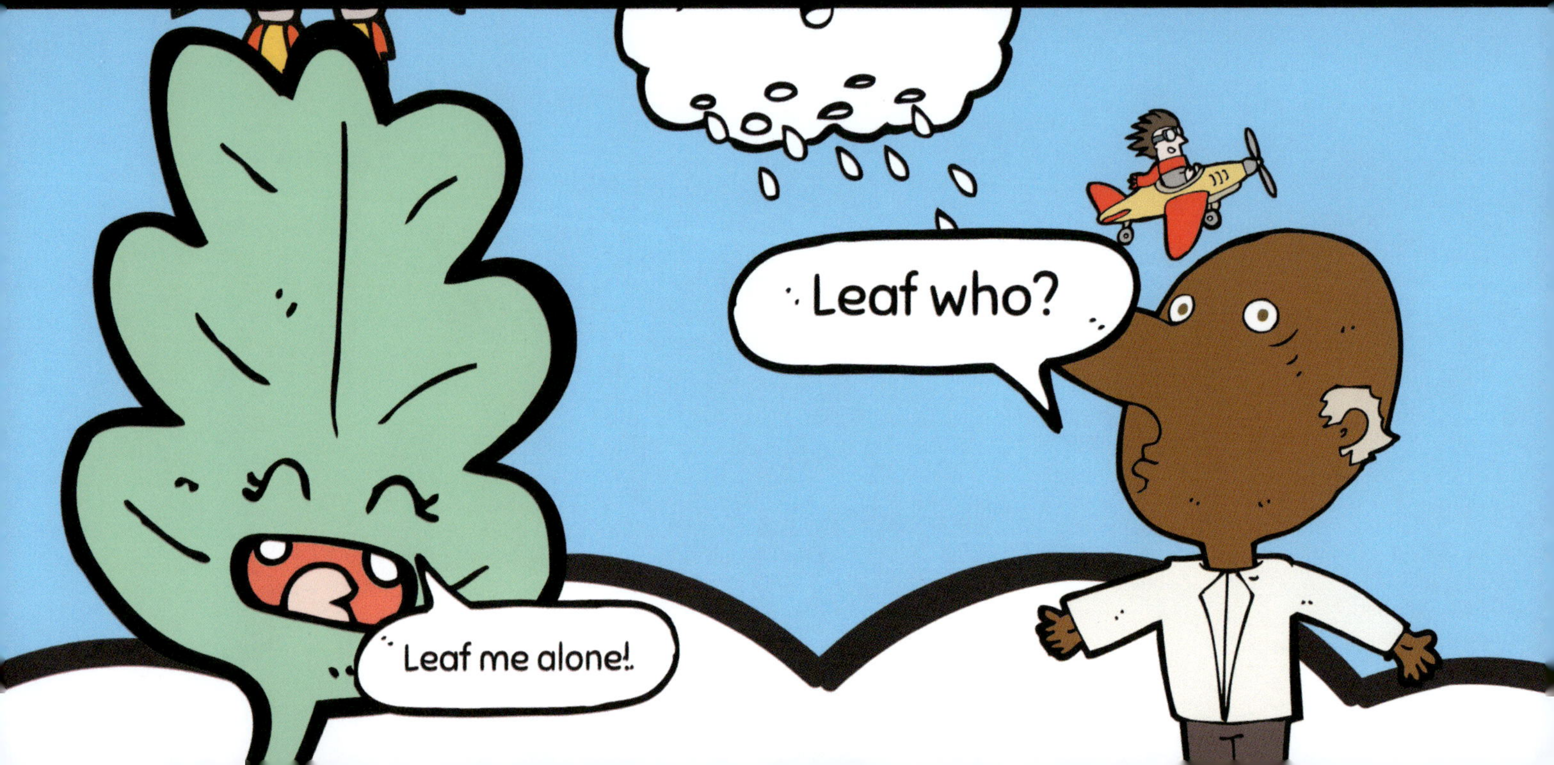
Leaf who?
Leaf me alone!

Q. Why did the kid throw the clock out the window?

A) Because he wanted to see time fly!

Q. What do you call cheese that is not yours?

A) Nacho cheese!

Q. Why did the pony get sent to his room?

A) Because he wouldn't stop horsing around!

Q. What do you call a bear with no ears?

A) A "B!"

Q. Which hand is better to write with?

A) Neither! It is better to write with a pencil!

Q. What animal can you always find at a baseball game?

A) A bat!

Q. If a seagull fly's over the sea, what fly's over the bay?

A) A bagel!

Q. Why did the cookie go to the doctor?

A) Because he felt crummy!

Knock, knock.
Who's there?
Goat.
Goat who?
Goat to the door and find out.

Q. How do you make an octopus laugh?

A) With ten-tickles!

LOL

Q. Where do pencils come from?

A) Penci-lvania!

Q. What's a monster's favourite game?

A) Swallow the leader!

Q. Why did the scientist wear denim?

A) Because he was a jean-ius!

Q. Who granted the fish a wish?

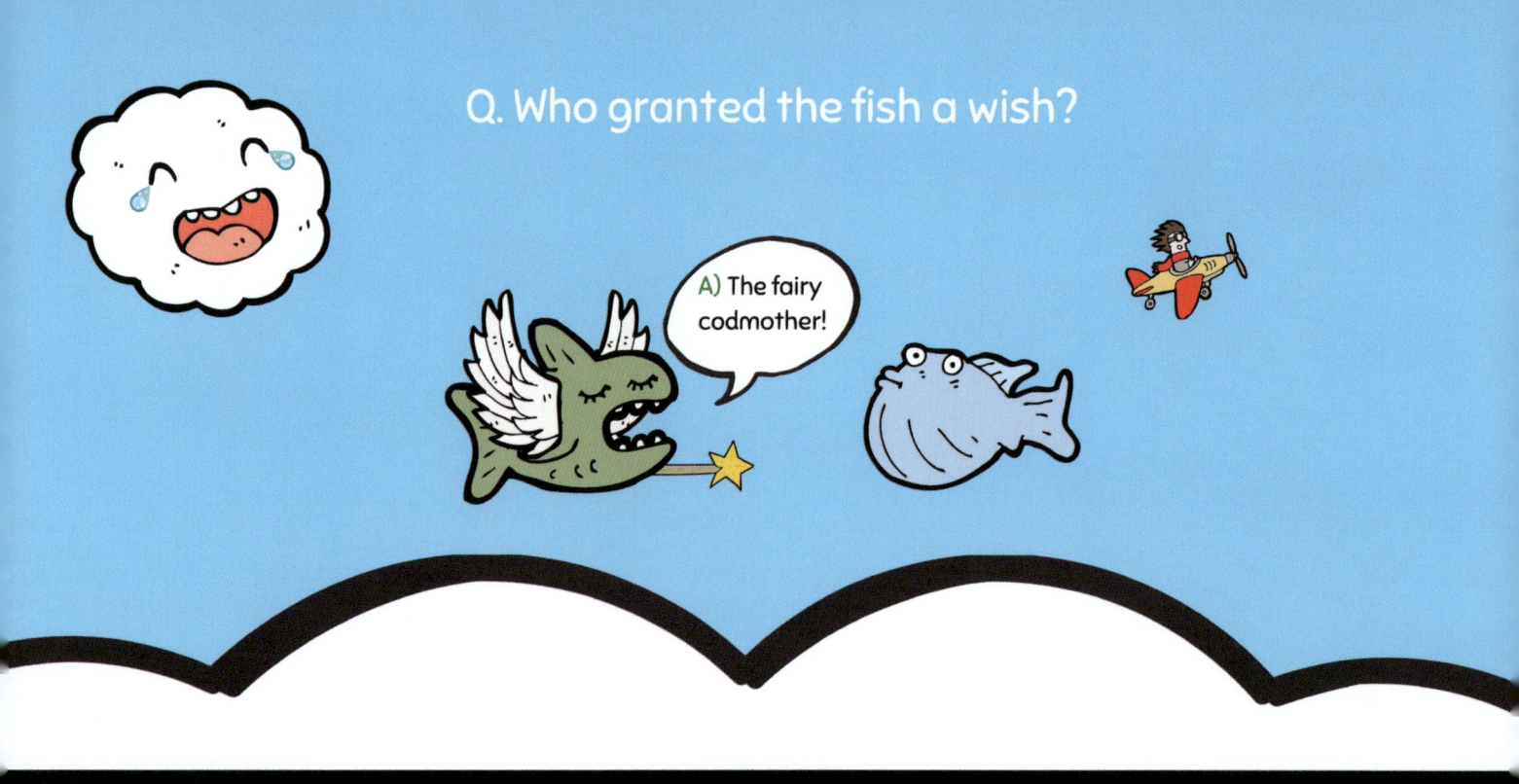

A) The fairy codmother!

Q. What wobbles in the sky?

A) A jellycopter!

Q. Why did the toilet paper roll down the hill?

A) To get to the bottom!

Q. Why did the burglar take a shower?

A) He wanted to make a clean getaway.!

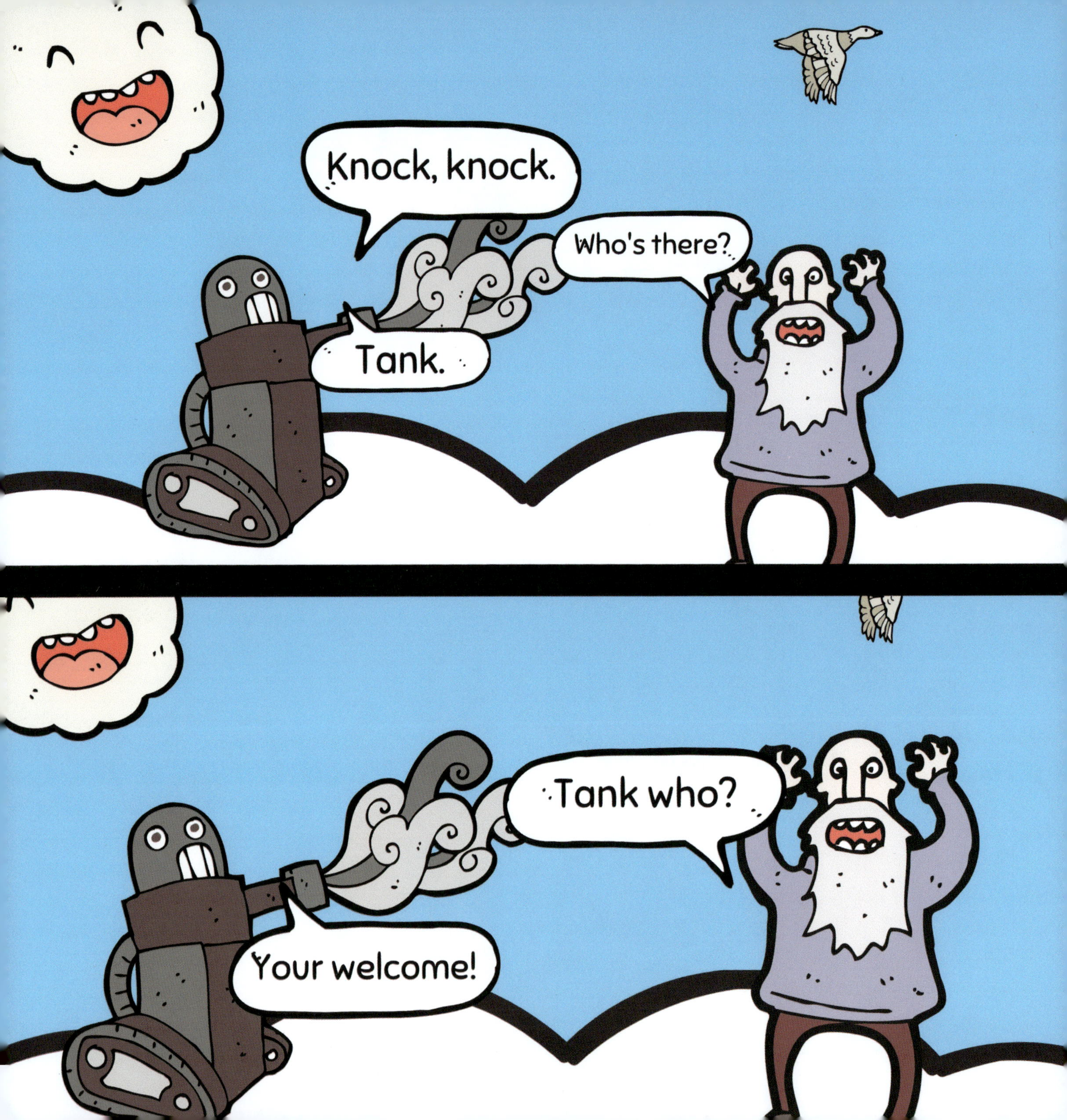
Knock, knock.
Who's there?
Tank.
Tank who?
Your welcome!

Knock, knock.
Who's there?
Ivan.
Ivan who?

Ivan to know if you enjoyed my jokes? Let me know by leaving a review on Amazon!

Follow this link to leave a review!

amazon.co.uk/review/create-review?asin=B091V288Y4&

or scan →

THE ULTIMATE KIDS JOKE BOOK COLLECTION

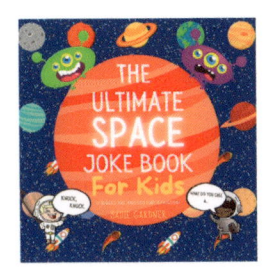

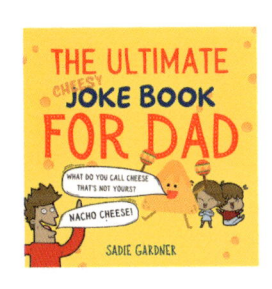

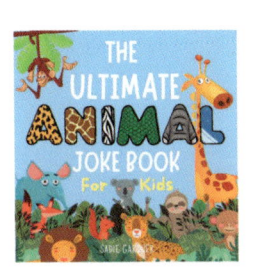

amazon.co.uk/dp/B08YM7HM91

or scan →

Printed in Great Britain
by Amazon